GREAT ART THEFTS

CHARLOTTE GUILLAIN

Raintree is an imprint of Capstone Global Library Limited, a company incorporated in England and Wales having its registered office at 7 Pilgrim Street, London, EC4V 6LB – Registered company number: 6695582

To contact Raintree please phone 0845 6044371, fax + 44 (0) 1865 312263, or email myorders@ raintreepublishers.co.uk. Customers from outside the UK please telephone +44 1865 312262.

Text © Capstone Global Library Limited 2013
First published in paperback in 2013
The moral rights of the proprietor have been asserted.

Edited by Laura Knowles, Adam Miller, Harriet Milles, and Helen Cox Cannons
Designed by Victoria Allen
Original illustrations © Capstone Global Library Ltd 2013
Illustrated by Martin Bustamante
Picture research by Tracy Cummins
Originated by Capstone Global Library Ltd
Production by Alison Parsons
Printed and bound in China by Leo Paper Products Ltd 2013

ISBN 978 1 406 24967 5
16 15 14 13 12
10 9 8 7 6 5 4 3 2 1

British Library Cataloguing in Publication Data

Guillain, Charlotte.
Great art thefts. -- (Treasure hunters)
364.1'6287-dc23
A full catalogue record for this book is available from the British Library.

Acknowledgements

We would like to thank the following for permission to reproduce photographs:
Alamy pp.11 (©Mary Evans Picture Library), 27 top (©GL Archive), 29 (©Linn Arvidsson), 37 (©Alistair Laming), 39 (©Peter Barritt); AP Photo pp.17 bot (©Josh Reynolds), 22 bot (©LISA POOLE); Art Resources p.35 top (©The Art Archive/Ashmolean Museum); Corbis pp.4 (©Sean Justice), 7 (©Hulton-Deutsch Collection, 8, 14, 18 (©Bettmann), 17 top (©Burstein Collection), 19 (©Atlantide Phototravel), 40 (©ARND WIEGMANN/ Reuters); Everett Collection p. 41 (©20th Century Fox Film Corp); Getty Images p.5 (©Oli Scarff), 6 (©Whitworth Art Gallery), 9 bot (©Popperfoto), 25 (©TEK IMAGE), 27 bot (©Maurice ROUGEMONT/ Gamma-Rapho), 30 (©HO/AFP), 31 (©AFP PHOTO/ SCANPIX/POLICE), 33 bot (©POPPE, CORNELIUS/ AFP), 43 (©PATRICK BAZ/AFP); ©Isabella Stewart Gardner Museum p.23; Newscom p.10 top (©OLYMPIA/SIPA); Shutterstock pp.9 top (©Studio38), 10 bot (©alexcoolok), 15 (©Matthew Jacques), 22 top (©Carsten Reisinger), 24 top (©Andy Dean Photography), 24 bot (©etraveler), 28 (©Africa Studio), 32 (©aboikis), 33 top (©RTimages), 36 (©R. Gino Santa Maria), 42 (©Fotovika); Superstock pp. 35 bot, 12 (©Exotica im/Exotica). Design features: Shutterstock.

Cover photographs reproduced with permission of Shutterstock (©DimkaSL/©Mr. Xu Ta Ku Pu/ ©Nina Malyna/©Serr Novik).

Expert consultant
We would like to thank Catherine Schofield Sezgin for her invaluable help in the preparation of this book. Catherine Sezgin has a master's degree in International Art Crime Studies and is the editor of the ARCAblog for the Association for Research into Crimes against Art.

CONTENTS

VALUABLE BUT VULNERABLE

Have you ever visited a museum or gallery to see a famous work of art? Or maybe you've heard of paintings such as the *Mona Lisa*, which are known around the world? What makes these paintings so special?

Many famous artists didn't make much money when they were alive. But sometimes certain painters' or sculptors' work can become very well known and valuable. Museums and collectors will pay millions of pounds for a single work of art.

Most museums and galleries hire security guards to protect the works of art.

LOOK BUT DON'T TOUCH!

How can galleries protect pictures hanging on the wall?

- Guards often stand near valuable art.

- Security cameras and alarms alert museums if a robbery is taking place.

- The frames around paintings can be bolted to the wall so they're hard to remove.

But even with these security measures, a painting can be easy to steal! It's right in front of the thief. Paintings don't weigh much once they've been cut out of a frame, so they are easy to transport and hide.

Large, heavy works of art, such as sculptures, can be stolen, too. In 2011, a bronze sculpture by Barbara Hepworth worth £500,000 was stolen from a park in London. Police think the thieves wanted to melt it down and sell the metal.

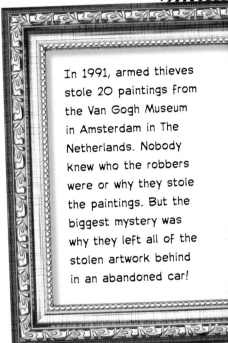

In 1991, armed thieves stole 20 paintings from the Van Gogh Museum in Amsterdam in The Netherlands. Nobody knew who the robbers were or why they stole the paintings. But the biggest mystery was why they left all of the stolen artwork behind in an abandoned car!

WHY STEAL ART?

Obviously many thieves steal art because it can be worth so much money. But in some unusual cases thieves take art for other reasons. Some robberies take place just to show how bad a gallery's security system is!

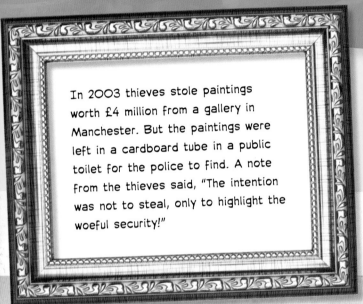

In 2003 thieves stole paintings worth £4 million from a gallery in Manchester. But the paintings were left in a cardboard tube in a public toilet for the police to find. A note from the thieves said, "The intention was not to steal, only to highlight the woeful security!"

This painting by Paul Gauguin was one of three stolen in the 2003 robbery.

STOLEN ART FOR SALE?

It might be easy for a professional thief to steal valuable art, but it's not so easy to sell it. Databases on the Internet alert galleries and law-abiding collectors around the world so they know if art has been stolen. Some art thieves make money out of the stolen works by holding them to ransom. They demand money from the gallery or owner in order for the art to be returned safely. Sometimes stolen art is used by criminal gangs to make deals and loans with other criminals.

Sometimes works of art are stolen during wars. During World War II, the Nazis famously stole art from Jewish art collectors and galleries in the countries they invaded. Some works were given to high-ranking officials and others were sold. After the war most of the art was not found because it was hidden. Even today many families are trying to reclaim their stolen art.

MISSING MONA LISA

It is early on an August morning in Paris. One of the world's finest art museums, the Louvre, is closed for cleaning. An unseen intruder heads directly to the world-famous painting, the *Mona Lisa*. The thief lifts the painting from its frame and sneaks out of the building. When the robbery is discovered, newspaper headlines around the world scream the news: the *Mona Lisa* has been stolen!

LEONARDO DA VINCI

Born: 1452

Died: 1519

Nationality: Italian

Profession: Renaissance artist, scientist, and inventor

Leonardo da Vinci painted the *Mona Lisa*. The painting is on a wooden board and is a portrait of a wealthy Italian merchant's wife, Lisa del Giocondo.

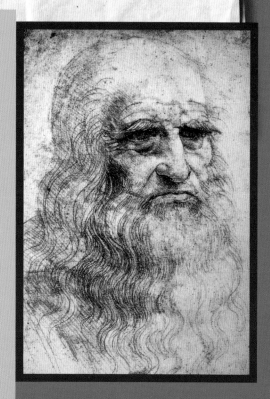

NOBODY NOTICED!

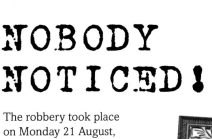

The robbery took place on Monday 21 August, 1911. Incredibly, nobody noticed the painting was missing until the next day! An artist came to the Louvre to copy the *Mona Lisa* and saw it was gone. When he asked about it, the guards assumed it was being cleaned. Finally, the museum authorities realized it had been stolen. The police hurried to the Louvre, which was shut and searched for a week. But the painting had vanished.

The Louvre in Paris is one of the most famous art galleries in the world.

This theft took place before security cameras and alarms protected art in galleries. The thief hid in the Louvre overnight so he could take the painting unseen. The painting had been in a glass case but it was only attached to the wall by four hooks. Nobody saw or heard a thing as he took the painting. The police could only come up with theories about what had happened.

A MYSTERY

The *Mona Lisa* was already world-famous before it was stolen. But after the theft, the painting became incredibly famous. People were so curious about the missing artwork that they queued up just to look at the space on the wall where the painting had hung! Several large rewards were offered to anyone who could help find it.

Two years passed and the police were still unable to trace the painting. They followed up suspects but each investigation led nowhere. Everyone wondered what the thief could do with such a famous painting? Why would they steal it? People also wondered how the thief had got the painting out of the Louvre without being seen. The *Mona Lisa* was small but heavy, and painted on slabs of wood that would be hard to hide. It was a mystery.

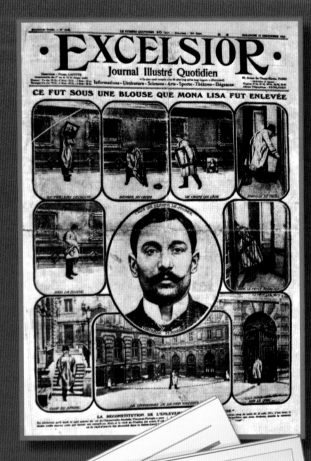

NEW YORK TIMES

24TH AUGUST 1911
60 DETECTIVES SEEK
STOLEN "MONA LISA"
BUT NO CLUE HAS YET BEEN
DISCOVERED AS TO WHEREABOUTS
OF LEONARDO'S MASTERPIECE.

Fingerprints

In 1911, police had just started using fingerprinting to trace criminals. One of the thief's thumbprints was on the glass case that had protected the *Mona Lisa*. But it was a left thumbprint and the police only kept a record of right thumbprints! Today, fingerprints are stored on computer records and they can be matched to criminals very quickly. But only people who have already been arrested have their fingerprints on file, so new criminals cannot be found this way.

Many people came to see the space on the wall where the *Mona Lisa* had hung.

MYSTERIOUS SMILE

Many people think that the *Mona Lisa* is mysterious. Wherever you stand, the woman in the painting always seems to be looking directly at you. It's also not clear whether she is smiling or not. Da Vinci used a painting technique called *sfumato*, blurring the edges of her mouth so it is hard to see if she is smiling. What do you think?

MONA LISA FOUND!

In 1913, an Italian man called Vincenzo Peruggia wrote to Alfredo Geri, an art and antiques dealer in Florence, Italy. Peruggia told Geri he wanted to sell him the *Mona Lisa* and return the painting to Italy. Geri arranged to meet Peruggia in Florence but he took an art expert to see the painting, thinking it must be a fake.

Peruggia waited in a hotel while Geri and the expert checked the painting. The expert was able to look at the cracking of the paint, called *craquelure*, to confirm that this really was the *Mona Lisa*. They immediately called the police and Peruggia was arrested.

False leads

Before the painting was found, there were many theories and leads, all of which led to nothing. Suspects included the painter Pablo Picasso, a wealthy American art collector, and a poet. Some thought the painting had been destroyed or taken to South America.

THIEF OR HERO?

Vincenzo Peruggia had kept the *Mona Lisa* hidden for over two years in his room in the Paris boarding house where he lived before taking it to Florence. He insisted his motive had been to return the painting to Italy, but police found evidence that he had already tried to sell it several times, without success.

VINCENZO PERUGGIA

Born: *1881*

Died: *1925*

Nationality: *Italian*

Profession: *former Louvre employee turned art thief*

ITALIAN ICON

Whether Peruggia's patriotic story was true or not, the painting did in fact tour several Italian cities after it was discovered. Many Italians thought Peruggia was a national hero for bringing the painting home, and he only served a few months in prison. However, the *Mona Lisa* eventually returned to Paris in 1914 and is still hanging in the Louvre today. Peruggia helped to make it one of the most iconic paintings in the world, and millions of visitors go to see the *Mona Lisa* each year.

Many people visit the Louvre just to see the *Mona Lisa*.

The *Mona Lisa* hasn't stayed peacefully in the Louvre since it was recovered. During World War II it was taken to several locations to keep it safe. Then in 1956 a visitor threw acid at the painting, damaging the lower section. Another visitor threw a rock at it! Since then, bulletproof glass has protected the *Mona Lisa* from other attacks.

BOSTON BURGLARY

It is the early hours of the morning on 18 March, 1990. St Patrick's Day parties are still going on all over the city of Boston. As the streets get quieter, a guard in the Isabella Stewart Gardner Museum hears a buzz at the door. Two men dressed as police officers ask him to let them in so they can check out a disturbance in the museum grounds. Unsuspecting, he lets them in and they ask him to move away from the counter, and the only alarm button.

When he calls the other guard, they are both handcuffed and tied up in the basement. Then the thieves begin taking paintings from the galleries. By 2.45 a.m. the thieves have left the building – having stolen 13 artworks, valued at more than US$300 million (£192 million). They have carried out the largest-ever single property theft.

ISABELLA STEWART GARDNER

Born: 1840

Died: 1924

Nationality: American

Profession: wealthy patron of the arts

For decades the empty frames where the stolen paintings once hung have remained on the walls of the Gardner Museum. This is because Isabella Stewart Gardner requested in her will that nothing should be moved or changed in the museum.

A HUGE LOSS

The robbers spent just over an hour taking paintings from various galleries in the Gardner Museum. The museum's motion detection system recorded where they went and shows how organized they were. The 13 items they took included paintings by famous artists Rembrandt, Vermeer (shown below), Manet, and Degas. The thieves removed the paintings from their frames quite roughly and may have caused serious damage.

The security guards were found in the basement at 8.15 a.m. They were able to describe the thieves to police but the guards were never shown any photographs of possible suspects.

Later, the guard who let the robbers in to the museum admitted that, looking back, he could tell that the intruders' moustaches were obviously fake!

WANTED
SUSPECT 1

AGE: late 30s
HEIGHT: 5 feet 9 inches (1.75 metres)

Slim build, gold wire glasses, moustache

WANTED
SUSPECT 2

AGE: early 30s
HEIGHT: 6 feet (1.83 metres)

Heavy build, moustache

Vulnerable security

The security alarms in the museum only warned guards if visitors got too close to artworks. They didn't alert police of a robbery. The thieves set off an alarm but easily found and destroyed it. A video camera recorded them entering the building, but the robbers easily removed the videotape as they left. Security is much tighter today.

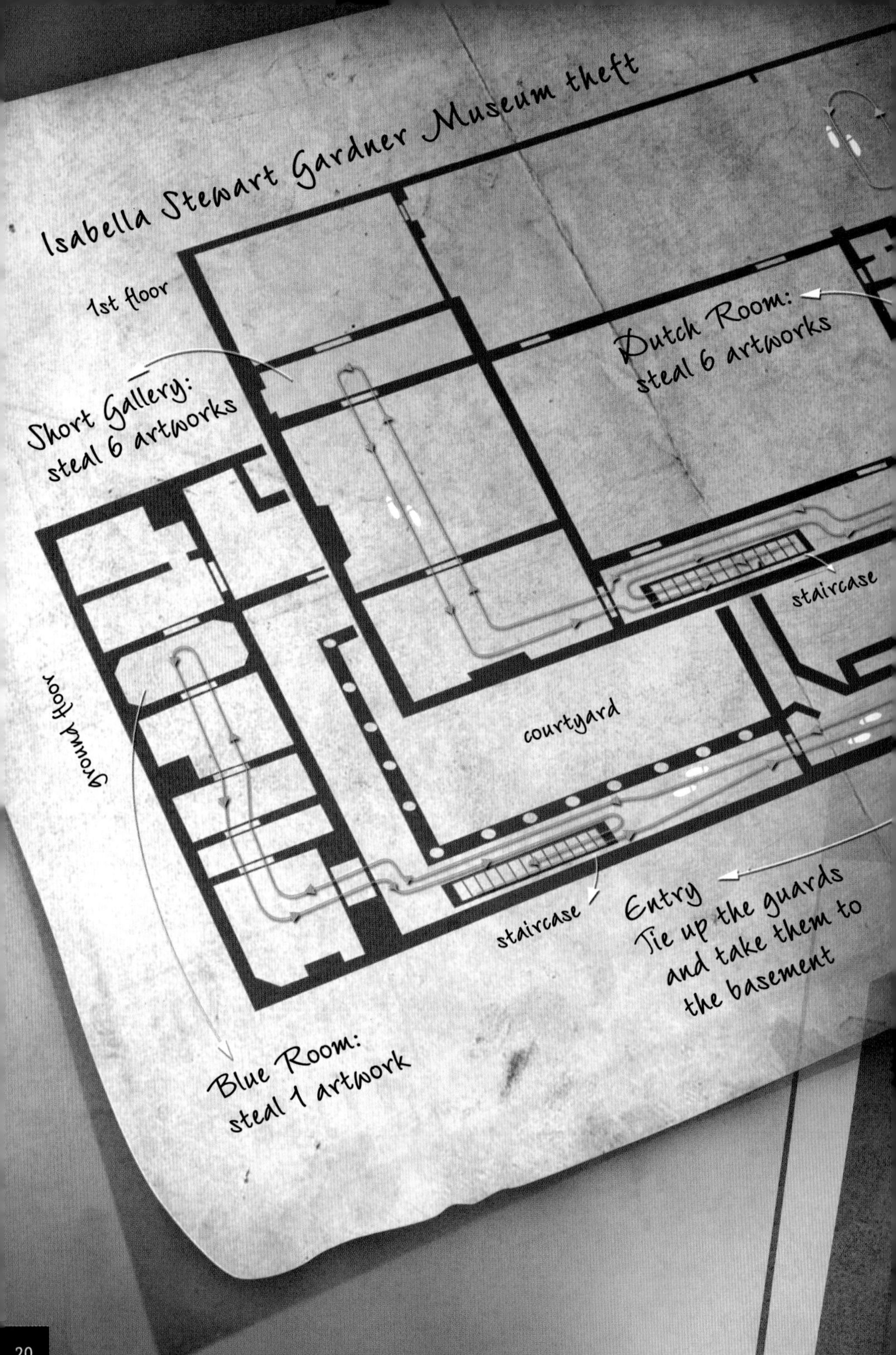

Isabella Stewart Gardner Museum theft

1st floor

Short Gallery:
steal 6 artworks

Dutch Room:
steal 6 artworks

staircase

ground floor

courtyard

staircase

Entry
Tie up the guards
and take them to
the basement

Blue Room:
steal 1 artwork

20

Escape

THEFT THEORIES

Nobody knows why the Gardner Museum paintings were taken. When the thieves left the guards, they told them the museum should expect a ransom demand for the stolen artwork. But no demand was ever made. The robbery had been carefully planned, as the museum's security weaknesses were targeted. Some people wondered whether a wealthy art dealer had arranged for the paintings to be stolen to order, but police think this is unlikely. The artwork was probably taken to be used in deals between criminal gangs.

WHO DID IT?

Boston police have never traced the criminals. Suspects have included the gangster James "Whitey" Bulger, the known criminal Thomas "Slab" Murphy, and notorious art thieves such as Myles Connor. Bulger was captured in 2011 but to date the crime remains unsolved, and many experts believe Bulger was not involved in this theft.

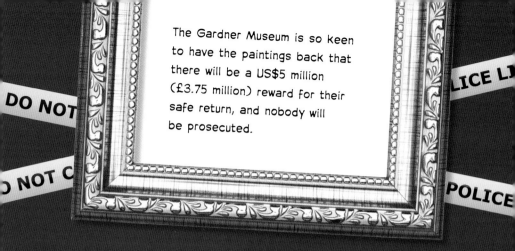

The Gardner Museum is so keen to have the paintings back that there will be a US$5 million (£3.75 million) reward for their safe return, and nobody will be prosecuted.

ANTHONY AMORE

Born: 1967

Nationality: American

Profession: Director of Security at the Isabella Stewart Gardner Museum

Anthony Amore worked in aviation security for the US government before taking charge of security at the Gardner Museum. He is working to trace the missing paintings and protect the museum's remaining collection.

"IF WE EVER SPEAK TO THE THIEVES . . . I WOULD LIKE TO SAY, 'WHY DID YOU TAKE THAT? WHY DID YOU PASS BY THE RAPHAEL?'"

ANTHONY AMORE, WHO WONDERS WHY THE THIEVES DIDN'T TAKE MORE VALUABLE PAINTINGS FROM THE GARDNER MUSEUM

OTHER LEADS

In 1994, a letter was sent to the Gardner Museum. The anonymous writer suggested the paintings could be returned in exchange for a US$2.6 million (£1.64 million) reward and immunity for all involved in the theft. The museum passed the letter to the FBI.

The person who sent the letter claimed the paintings were being kept carefully. The museum was instructed to show if they were willing to consider paying a ransom by putting a coded message in the *Boston Sunday Globe* newspaper.

Then a second letter was sent. The letter writer suspected the police were getting involved and warned that the paintings would not be returned if there was a danger that he would be arrested. He asked for time to think but suggested that he might send some information about the paintings' location. He was never heard from again.

Cutting-edge security

Since the robbery, video surveillance and recording technology have vastly improved. Now the museum could capture an image of an intruder from any number of angles, even in complete darkness. The best security technology has also been installed, so even if a thief got through one level of security, another would remain in place.

DNA

Police are hoping that developments in DNA testing may help them trace the Gardner Museum thieves. Evidence from the crime scene may give officers new information about the robbers' identities. Today's technology could take a sample of skin or hair and tell police about the person's appearance. They could also search a DNA database that could pinpoint the criminals.

STEALING THE SCREAM

It is 12 February, 1994, and celebrations are taking place across Norway as the Winter Olympics open in Lillehammer.

In the early hours of the morning, dark figures climb a ladder outside the National Art Museum in Oslo. The silence is broken as a window smashes and the intruders enter the museum. As security alarms alert police, the thieves use wire cutters to remove a world-famous painting called *The Scream* by Edvard Munch from the wall. By the time the police arrive, the robbers have gone, taking one of the most famous paintings in the world.

EASY PICKINGS

Despite the police arriving at the museum within minutes, it had been relatively easy for the robbers to get in and take the painting quickly. They even left a note behind saying, "Thanks for the poor security". The museum had moved the painting to a different gallery as part of the Olympic celebrations, and this may have left it less secure than normal. However, the thieves were recorded on security cameras.

EDVARD MUNCH

Born: 1863

Died: 1944

Nationality: Norwegian

Edvard Munch painted, drew, and printed several versions of *The Scream*. He suffered from unhappiness and mental illness. Many people think that *The Scream* shows Munch's despair and anxiety about life.

Edvard Munch later said that he was almost mad at the time he painted *The Scream*.

LOST AND FOUND

Following the robbery, a ransom note for US$1 million (£630,000) was sent to the Norwegian government. But it was impossible to know who sent it, and the ransom was not paid. Instead, Norwegian police worked with British detectives to set up a sting operation to catch the thieves. Officers worked undercover and their investigations led to the arrest of four men. Luckily the painting itself was not damaged.

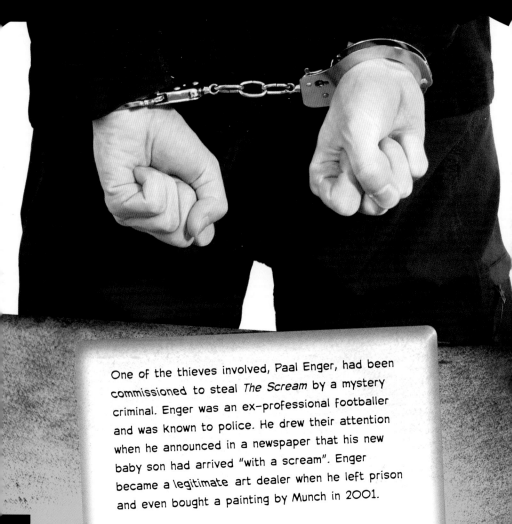

One of the thieves involved, Paal Enger, had been commissioned to steal *The Scream* by a mystery criminal. Enger was an ex-professional footballer and was known to police. He drew their attention when he announced in a newspaper that his new baby son had arrived "with a scream". Enger became a legitimate art dealer when he left prison and even bought a painting by Munch in 2001.

CHARLEY HILL

Born: 1947

Nationality: British

Profession: ex-police officer who tracks down stolen art

Charley Hill played a key role in tracking down *The Scream* in 1994. He worked undercover, pretending to be a representative from the Getty Museum in California. He told the thieves the Getty Museum would buy the painting back from them and in return Norway would loan the painting to the Getty.

"MOST ART COLLECTIONS ARE VERY BADLY PROTECTED. THE REASON IS, THEY'RE ON PUBLIC DISPLAY... THE THIEVES ARE TOLD THE THINGS ARE WORTH A FORTUNE, THAT THEY'RE RELATIVELY EASY TO STEAL, SO THEY STEAL – THEN THEY HAVE TO GET RID OF THEM."

CHARLEY HILL, STOLEN ART DETECTIVE

Today, Munch's house is a tourist attraction.

SCREAM AGAIN!

Fast-forward to 2004. On a quiet Sunday morning in August, two men run in to the Munch Museum in Oslo, Norway. One of the masked thieves waves his gun in the air as another version of *The Scream* is pulled off the gallery wall. On the way out they take another painting by Munch, *The Madonna*. Together the paintings are worth around £12 million.

Police in front of the Munch Museum after the robbery.

ANY EVIDENCE?

The theft was caught on security cameras, but the robbers' black hoods made it impossible to identify them. Electronic tracking devices were attached to the frames of the paintings, but it was easy for the robbers to rip these off as they left the museum. *The Scream* was quite badly damaged when they did this.

Police found the getaway car 16 kilometres (10 miles) away from the museum. However, the robbers had sprayed the car all over with foam from a fire extinguisher, so any fingerprints or DNA evidence were washed away. The museum was closed for ten months after the robbery.

Photographs were taken of the robbers as they escaped with the paintings.

When the thieves arrived at the museum wearing balaclavas and hoods, they ran into a glass door! They had to pick themselves up and wait for the door to slide open. Once inside, they weren't sure where to go and changed direction several times before asking someone to show them where the painting was!

THOMAS NATAAS

Nationality: Norwegian

Profession: Drag racer

Nataas owned a bus that he lived in when he travelled to drag races around Europe. The robbers stored the stolen paintings in his bus shortly after the theft – against Nataas's will.

THEFT THEORIES

Norwegian police followed up several leads but they didn't trace the paintings to Thomas Nataas's bus until they had been removed and taken elsewhere. Pressure was coming from all over the world for the paintings to be found. Rumours spread that the paintings had been destroyed or taken far away by Russian organized crime gangs.

However, the police believed the thieves were Norwegian and were probably known to them. They thought the robbery had been staged to divert attention from a recent bank robbery, when a police officer had been killed.

"IT WAS NOT VERY PROFESSIONAL; THEY HADN'T DONE THEIR HOMEWORK VERY WELL. THERE WAS CONFUSION ABOUT WHERE THE PAINTING WAS ... THIS GAVE US SOMETHING TO THINK ABOUT."

IVER STENSRUD, A NORWEGIAN POLICE CHIEF, COMMENTING ON THE CASE.

CONNECTION MADE

DAVID TOSKA

Date of Birth: 1975

Nationality: Norwegian

Profession: bank robber

Toska was convicted for masterminding the bank robbery in Stavanger, Norway in April 2004, when a police officer was murdered. He is thought to have arranged for *The Scream* to be stolen to distract police from this crime.

In April 2005, several people were arrested for the bank robbery and murder. As they were sentenced, an anonymous tip-off was given to police, telling them where to find the paintings. In August 2006, Ingebørg Ydstie, chief curator of the Munch Museum, was taken by police to identify two paintings in a van. *The Scream* and *The Madonna* had been found!

NEW YEAR'S THEFT

People around the world are celebrating the start of the new millennium. As the year 2000 begins and fireworks are set off in a noisy display, a thief is stealthily climbing up scaffolding outside the Ashmolean Museum in Oxford. Under the cover of darkness, he opens a skylight and lowers himself into the building on a rope ladder.

As security alarms begin to sound, the robber sets off a smoke canister that starts the fire alarm and blocks the view of security cameras. Then he calmly cuts a painting worth £3 million (US$4.8 million) from its frame and climbs out of the museum.

NOT INSURED

The stolen artwork was *View of Auvers-sur-Oise*, by the French Impressionist painter Cézanne. Like many great works of art kept in public galleries, it was not insured against theft. This is usually because the cost of the insurance would be too expensive. Paintings can be insured against damage from fire or water as they can often be repaired, but once a painting is stolen it can't be replaced.

A smoke canister is a type of firework that produces a smokescreen when it is lit. It is often used by the military, or in games such as paintballing.

This is the *View of Auvers-sur-Oise*. The painting was never finished – Cézanne never signed or dated it.

PAUL CÉZANNE

Born: 1839

Died: 1906

Nationality: French

Profession: artist

Cézanne was an important painter at the end of the 19th century. His work moved from Impressionism towards the Cubism of the 20th Century.

CONFUSION

Many people had expected problems with computers and alarm systems when the year 2000 began. When the robber set off the Ashmolean's fire alarms using the smoke canister and a fan, a porter at the museum called the fire brigade rather than suspecting theft.

The authorities only realized that the Cézanne painting was missing when firefighters discovered the empty smoke canister. By then the thief was long gone. He had worn gloves to avoid leaving fingerprints as evidence. This professional art thief had known exactly which painting to take and where to find it.

"WHOEVER HAS TAKEN THIS PAINTING HAS GIVEN SOME THOUGHT TO HOW TO STEAL IT. THE PERSON HAS SOME REASON FOR IT, AND SOME OUTLET FOR IT. ONE POSSIBILITY IS IT HAS BEEN STOLEN TO ORDER."

SUPERINTENDENT JOHN CARR OF OXFORD POLICE.

POLICE RESPONSE

The police were quickly aware that this was not a normal crime. One spokesperson said, "This is not a crime which is going to be solved overnight. We are more used to run-of-the-mill crimes. We need expertise."

Authorities at ports and airports were alerted to the theft in case the thief tried to take the painting out of the country. The police also appealed to any possible witnesses who may have been celebrating New Year on the streets of Oxford and seen the thief make his escape.

FBI top ten art crimes

The Ashmolean Museum theft is in the FBI's top ten art crimes. This list also includes the paintings stolen from the Gardner Museum, a Van Gogh painting, and artefacts stolen from museums in Iraq.

A NEW LEAD?

As the police searched for leads, art experts grew concerned that the Cézanne painting might have been badly damaged when it was cut from its frame. They also worried that the painting could be damaged if it was not kept in a controlled atmosphere. Detectives were under pressure to trace the painting.

The police explored the idea that criminals had stolen the painting to order. In January 2000, they received a tip-off that the painting was in a pub in the city of Coventry, about 90 kilometres (50 miles) from Oxford. But when police raided the pub, they discovered the painting was a copy painted by the landlord! The police had other leads from many callers giving information, but the painting was still not found.

Security improvements

Since the theft, the Ashmolean Museum has tightened its security. In 2009 the museum was renovated, and improved security was an important part of the building's new design. Cutting-edge physical and electronic security, plus improved CCTV coverage, has been installed throughout the museum. All museums and galleries can take action to improve security, but there are limits to what they can do to prevent theft when art is displayed in public.

"THIS IS A VERY, VERY LARGE BUILDING. UNLESS YOU CAN PUT STAFF IN EVERY GALLERY EVERY NIGHT, HOW CAN YOU DEAL WITH THIS?"

DR CHRISTOPHER BROWN, DIRECTOR OF THE ASHMOLEAN MUSEUM. THE YEAR BEFORE THE THEFT, THE MUSEUM HAD BEEN GIVEN AN A1 RATING BY A SECURITY ADVISOR.

WHERE DO THE PAINTINGS GO?

Criminal gangs who are involved in activities such as drug smuggling and money laundering are often responsible for organizing some types of "made-to-order" art theft. If they don't try to get money from museums and galleries through a ransom, then they use the stolen art as a guarantee when they make deals with each other.

TRACKING DOWN STOLEN ART

The Cézanne painting and other unsolved art thefts are recorded on the Art Loss Register. This organization works with the authorities around the world to find stolen art. The international police organization Interpol also has a Stolen Art Database. These registers publish lists of stolen works of art, which makes it impossible for the thieves to sell them on the open market. This means they can only try to pass on stolen artworks illegally – and would never be able to sell them for their true value.

Stolen art could never be sold at a legal art auction.

Advances online

The Internet has become a useful tool in the fight against art theft. Images and details of stolen artworks can now be circulated around the world instantly, and it is easier for anyone with information on stolen art to contact the relevant authorities.

"THE PUBLIC ALWAYS SEEMS TO THINK THAT THESE WORKS OF ART ARE STOLEN TO FURNISH SOMEBODY'S YACHT BECAUSE THEY CAN'T LIVE WITHOUT A CÉZANNE. IT'S HIGHLY UNLIKELY. FAMOUS WORKS OF ART GET STOLEN BY CRIMINAL GANGS."

HUGO PENNING, HEAD OF SECURITY AT OXFORD'S ASHMOLEAN MUSEUM

PROTECTING ART

Museums and galleries around the world are vigilant in the fight against art thieves, and security has been improved dramatically since the *Mona Lisa* was stolen in 1911. Cameras and alarms are now effective ways of preventing crime and catching criminals. Computer technology helps to prevent works of art being stolen and to trace missing paintings.

MORE ART CRIMES

Unfortunately only so much can be done to protect art. A sad development in the world of art crime is the theft of metal sculptures in public places. These are then melted down so that the metal can be sold. These works of art can never be replaced.

Other robberies are virtually impossible to plan for. In 2002, over £630,000 worth of art was stolen from the National Fine Arts Museum in Asuncion, Paraguay. The robbers dug a 25-metre-long tunnel from a nearby shop to break into the museum undetected.

It is also hard to protect art when countries are in chaos or at war. In 2003, the Iraqi National Museum was left unprotected as the country was invaded. The museum was looted, and many priceless artefacts were stolen or destroyed. Most will never be recovered.

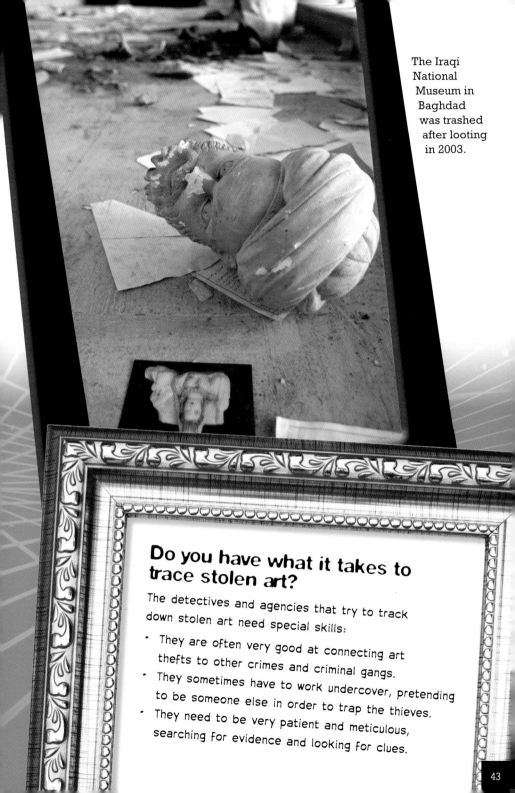

The Iraqi National Museum in Baghdad was trashed after looting in 2003.

Do you have what it takes to trace stolen art?

The detectives and agencies that try to track down stolen art need special skills:

- They are often very good at connecting art thefts to other crimes and criminal gangs.
- They sometimes have to work undercover, pretending to be someone else in order to trap the thieves.
- They need to be very patient and meticulous, searching for evidence and looking for clues.

TIMELINE

c.1503-1519
Leonardo da Vinci paints the *Mona Lisa*.

1879-1882
Paul Cézanne paints *View of Auvers-sur-Oise*.

1893
Edvard Munch paints the first version of *The Scream*.

1911
The *Mona Lisa* is stolen from the Louvre in Paris.

1913
The *Mona Lisa* is found in Florence. Vincenzo Peruggia is arrested.

1914
The *Mona Lisa* is returned to Paris.

1924
The wealthy American patron of the arts Isabella Stewart Gardner dies, leaving behind an art collection that the public can view.

1956
A visitor throws acid at the *Mona Lisa*, damaging the painting.

1990
The Isabella Stewart Gardner Museum is robbed, with 13 artworks valued at over US$300 million (£192 million) taken by the thieves.

1991
Armed thieves steal 20 paintings from the Van Gogh Museum in Amsterdam.

1994
A letter is sent to the Gardner Museum suggesting the stolen artworks could be returned in exchange for a ransom. This doesn't happen. *The Scream* is stolen from the National Art Museum in Oslo.

2000
The painting *View of Auvers-sur-Oise* by Paul Cézanne is stolen from the Ashmolean Museum in Oxford.

2002
Over £630,000 worth of art is stolen when thieves tunnel into the National Fine Arts Museum in Asuncion, Paraguay.

2003
Thieves steal paintings worth £4 million from a gallery in Manchester. They are later found in a public toilet.
The Iraqi National Museum in Baghdad is looted and countless priceless artefacts are lost.

2004
Another version of *The Scream* and another painting by Munch (*The Madonna*) are stolen from the Munch Museum in Oslo.

2006
The Scream and *The Madonna* are recovered.

2011
A sculpture by Barbara Hepworth worth £500,000 is stolen from a London park by suspected metal thieves. James "Whitey" Bulger, a suspect in the Isabella Stewart Gardner Museum robbery, is captured.

GLOSSARY

artefact art object made by humans, particularly from the past

commission pay someone for a service

Cubism early 20th century art style that used geometric shapes to represent objects, people, and landscapes

DNA testing technique used by scientists to identify people, using samples such as hair, blood, skin, or saliva that contain their DNA

drag racer driver who races a specially adapted car from a standing start

FBI (Federal Bureau of Investigation) the US government's security and law enforcement organization

fingerprinting technique used to identify people by the patterns on their fingerprints

gangster member of a criminal gang, usually violent

iconic something that is instantly recognized by most people and represents something important

immunity protection from something

Impressionist 19th century style of painting that suggested the mood of the subject using colour and light rather than lots of detail

legitimate legal

looting stealing things from a place, often during war or riot

meticulous doing something very slowly and carefully, with great attention to detail

money laundering methods used by criminals to hide the source of money they have gained through crime

motive reason behind someone's actions

Nazi member of the German National Socialist Party in the early 20th century, led by Adolf Hitler

organized crime networks of criminal gangs

patriotic full of love for your country

patron person who gives support and financial help

prosecute take legal action against someone

ransom money demanded by criminals for the safe return of a person or object

Renaissance revival of classical thinking and arts that began in Italy in the 14th century

renovate restore something to a better state

sting operation undercover operation designed to catch criminals

surveillance watching closely

suspect person thought to be guilty of a crime or offence

theory idea of how something has happened

will written document that outlines a person's wishes after their death

FIND OUT MORE

BOOKS

Introduction to Art, Rosie Dickins and Mari Griffith (Usborne, 2009)

Loot: Inside the World of Stolen Art, Thomas McShane and Dary Matera (Maverick House, 2007)

Mona Lisa: The History of the World's Most Famous Painting, Donald Sassoon (HarperCollins, 2009)

Stealing The Scream: The Hunt For a Missing Masterpiece, Edward Dolnick (Icon Books Ltd, 2008)

The Gardner Heist: The True Story of the World's Largest Unsolved Art Theft, Ulrich Boser (HarperPaperbacks, 2010)

The Impressionists, Freya Blackwood (Usborne Publishing, 2009)

WEBSITES

www.artloss.com/
Visit the Art Loss Register's website to find out more about their work.

www.ashmolean.org
Find out more about works of art at the Ashmolean Museum on this website.

www.gardnermuseum.org/
This website will tell you more about the Isabella Stewart Gardner Museum and includes information on the 1990 theft in its Resources section.

www.guardian.co.uk/artanddesign/art-theft
Find out more about art thefts in this special section of the Guardian newspaper's website.

www.louvre.fr/en
Visit the official website of the Louvre in Paris to find out more about the *Mona Lisa* and the many other priceless works of art in the museum.

www.munch.museum.no/content.aspx?id=151&mid=&lang=en
Visit this section of the Munch Museum website to see how art experts have tried to repair the damage done to *The Scream* and *The Madonna* after the 2004 theft.

Places to visit

The Ashmolean Museum
Beaumont Street
Oxford
OX1 2PH
UK

Isabella Stewart Gardner Museum
280 The Fenway
Boston
MA 02115
USA

The Louvre Museum
75058 Paris
France

The Munch Museum
Tøyengata
53 0578 Oslo
Norway

The Van Gogh Museum
Paulus Potterstraat 7
Amsterdam
The Netherlands

Topics for further research

Find out about another famous art theft that isn't described in this book. How did the thieves manage to steal the work of art? Has the art been found and, if so, what techniques did detectives use to trace it?

Visit an art museum or gallery where you live and look at the security that is in place to protect the artwork. Do you think the museum could do more to protect its art?

Choose one of the artists mentioned in this book and find out more about his or her life and works. Why do you think their work is worth so much money today?

INDEX